D1500071

DEDICATION

I would like to dedicate this book to my Father God, the Lord Jesus Christ, and the Holy Spirit.

I wish to acknowledge my loving Husband, Roddric and my wonderful daughters Briana and Eryn.

To my family, I would like to thank my parents, Henry and Dorothy Dorsey, for their continued love and support. To my younger brother, Hendrik, I am so grateful to have you in my life. To my family and friends for their love and support. I appreciate the amazing love and support from all divine helpers that God so gracefully placed along my way.

Think Like An Ant

A 14-Day Devotional Workbook on
Wisdom and Time Management

By
Madra Bell

This devotional belongs to:

_____

THE WORDS THAT SPARKED MY CURIOSITY

There are two Bible verses that ignited my interest in ants. Once I read them, I was inspired to find out why insects were highlighted in the Word of God. Take a look at what the scriptures said:

"Four things on earth are small, but they are exceedingly wise; the ants are a people not strong, yet they provide their food in the summer; " Proverbs 30:24-25

"Go to the ant, O sluggard; consider her ways, and be wise. Without having any chief, officer, or ruler, she prepares her bread in summer and gathers her food in harvest. How long will you lie there, O sluggard? When will you arise from your sleep? A little sleep, a little slumber, a little folding of the hands to rest. " Proverbs 6:6-11

These verses point to some powerful truths about this insect. When I meditated on those verses, I could not rest. I realized that God wanted believers to examine and adopt their habits. I researched their culture. What I learned was so amazing that I had to share it. Once I discovered how they could put the average person to shame, one question came to mind. How could I think more like an ant?

Join me in this 14 day devotional workbook to reflect on the wisdom and secrets of these resourceful creatures. I encourage you to write notes for the daily journal prompts. It will help you to grasp the principle for each day. Take the challenge at the end of the 14 days! Be sure to utilize the budget and vision planners located in the back of the workbook during the challenge. I pray it blesses your faith.

Wisdom from above will always assist people with supernatural achievement and time management. Leave it to God to make it as simple as watching how ants behave. Corinthians 1:27 says "But God has chosen the foolish things of the world to confound the wise. God has chosen the weak things of the world to confound the things which are mighty."

DAY 1

"Time is a resource that can be measured by
the sweat and tears poured into it. Only God
The Almighty can redeem it."

A study from Harvard and Florida State Universities revealed that ants first appeared around 130 million years ago. Ants know how to stand the test of time and are wise about its value. Ants work on a particular activity and stick to a schedule because they are extreme planners. They seem to know how to sense winter and summer seasons which is crucial for planning. They are very neat and extremely organized. They devise a plan for future use, gather resources and bring the resources back to the home front. They will use what they find for daily meals and winter storage. God also designed us to gather, share, enjoy and save resources. Wisdom cries for us to be prepared in season and out of season for ourselves and for our loved ones. Prayer and observation is needed for discernment of the seasons that we are in. We must know the proper time to work, share, use or save whatever we steward. It could be the difference between famine and feast in our lives.

Today's Scripture:

And the sun stood still, and the moon stayed, Until the nation had avenged themselves of their enemies. Is this not written in the book of Jashar? And the sun stayed in the midst of heaven, and hastened not to go down about a whole day.
Joshua 10:13

JOURNAL PROMPT

A PLAN AND A SCHEDULE TO EXECUTE THE
PLAN ARE THE FOUNDATION FOR SUCCESSFUL
TIME MANAGEMENT. DO YOU MAKE PLANS OR
SCHEDULES FOR IMPORTANT ACTIVITIES? WHAT
ARE SOME OF YOUR ABANDONED DREAMS OR
VISIONS IN WHICH YOU WANT GOD TO REDEEM
THE TIME FOR? RECORD YOUR THOUGHTS
BELOW.

"

Maximize Time. God is able to make the Miraculous happen in your plans.

DAY 2

"BIG VISIONS NEED BIG LADDERS AND DEPENDABLE HANDS"

Ants have big vision despite their size. They can build an ant hill as large as or even larger than a house. This implies they know exactly what they need and want. They know how to visualize and are ready to throw themselves fully into the vision. They focus all the energy into achieving their huge plan and are not intimidated by the magnitude of what it takes to accomplish the task. God also designed us to execute large visions. He always gives us a vision that is much bigger than we are and we must look to Him as well as our divine helpers to carry it out. Like the ant, we will need to focus a great deal of energy into achieving the plan. If we look at our abilities, we become intimidated by the magnitude of what is required, but we must remember that we are not alone in our efforts. Like the ant, we must rely on a reliable team of supporters. Evaluate your support. If there is no support, there is a missing part of the puzzle. Large dreams need large amounts of assistance. Pride will fight against this truth but remember to fight even harder to produce your divine dreams.

Today's Scripture:

"Whoever isolates himself seeks his own desire; he breaks out against all sound judgment." Proverbs 18:1

JOURNAL PROMPT

YOU NEED GOOD HELP. WHO CAN YOU LEAN ON
TO ASSIST YOU? HAVE YOU COMMITTED TO
PRAYING FOR DIVINE HELPERS TO ASSIST WITH
YOUR VISION? RECORD THOUGHTS OR PRAYERS
ON THE JOURNAL PAGE.

"Keep your eyes open. Surround yourself with sound judgment that comes from sound minds."

DAY 3

"When you value your gifts and abilities, dedication will eventually leak into your work ethic."

Ants are prone to work very hard. Ants can carry up to 50 times their own body weight. You will not find a spirit of laziness among them. Each member of the team knows the mission and works extremely hard to handle the responsibilities of the mission. If laziness was among their culture, they would struggle to meet their daily goals. King Solomon, one of the wisest persons that ever lived, directed lazy men to go to the ant and learn how to work diligently. If we were to take a lesson from them, we would adopt their way of striving to get our desires. A recent study showed that ants seem to prefer whichever treat they worked the hardest to get! This implies they value endurance and enjoy rewards to the degree of the challenge it takes to gain the reward. We can not be passive. We have to forsake laziness. Afterwards, we need to take pleasure in what we accomplish without the guilt trips that others may put on us.

Today's Scripture:

In all things I have shown you that by working hard in this way we must help the weak and remember the words of the Lord Jesus, how he himself said, "It is more blessed to give than to receive." Acts 20:35

JOURNAL PROMPT

HARD WORK COMES WITH THE TERRITORY.
YOUR CIRCLE NEEDS YOU. HAVE YOU
COMMITTED TO HELPING YOURSELF AND
THOSE AROUND YOU? RECORD YOUR
THOUGHTS ON THE JOURNAL PAGE.

"*If you Sow* into others you will reap from others."

"It is a Blessing to Give. It is an honor to serve."

Day 4

**"When life disturbs your footsteps along the path,
remember the reason you started the journey
in the first place."**

Ants are self-motivated creatures. They don't need encouragement to work for what is good and rewarding. They don't depend on leaders to boost morale. They value the assignment and encourage themselves to finish it. This shows that they are purpose driven and have a strong sense of direction. Thank God for great leaders, but in the event, you are under a leader that is still growing or developing, follow the footsteps of the ant and encourage yourself in your assignments. Pray and seek the Word for a strategy in the area that your leader needs assistance. Respectfully offer solutions and assistance. Remember why you do what you do to encourage yourself. The Bible mentioned that King David, King Solomon's Father, encouraged himself in the Lord. Sometimes if we don't have outside motivation, we need to pray and push not to give up. Find an assignment, a purpose and a vision that will keep you inspired to keep going. Know why you do what you do.

Today's Scripture:

Brothers do not be children in your thinking. Be infants in evil, but in your thinking be mature. 1 Corinthians 14:20

JOURNAL PROMPT

WHAT ARE SOME GOALS THAT YOU NEED TO BE
SELF-MOTIVATED ABOUT? RECORD YOUR
THOUGHTS ON THE JOURNAL PAGE.

Encourage

Yourself!

"Thoughts have the potential to turn into the things that dreams are made of.

Thoughts also can be the things that nightmares are made of. Choose Wisely."

DAY 5

"EVEN THE STRONGEST ONE IN THE CREW CAN USE A HELPING HAND TO MAKE PROGRESS".

Ants are surprisingly selfless creatures. They do not appear to be selfish. If one ant finds food, it gives signals to the others. If one ant finds another ant dead, it signals the others so that they may carry the corpse away as a group. Showing care for another's welfare requires self-control. If a human family or community wants to flourish, each member will need to display generosity. Envy, jealousy, strife and competition must be placed at the feet of Jesus. Supporting other team members is mandatory for the advancement of the team. It is all about service. Service is a seed that grows and blooms beautifully in God's Kingdom and in our communities.

Today's Scripture:

For you were called to freedom, brothers. Only do not use your freedom as an opportunity for the flesh, but through love serve one another. Galatians 5:13

JOURNAL PROMPT:

BANISH ALL SELFISH AMBITIONS TO RISE
HIGHER. WRITE ABOUT A TIME WHEN SOMEONE
HELPED YOU TO DO SOMETHING IMPORTANT.
HOW DID THEIR SELFLESSNESS INSPIRE YOU?
RECORD YOUR THOUGHTS ON THE JOURNAL
NOTES.

Progress *is in prayer!*

"When you are free, you set the wheels of change in motion for others around you."

DAY 6

"WE MUST FELLOWSHIP IN A SPIRIT OF KINDNESS. IT IS A CORNERSTONE OF UNITY."

Ants seem to greet each other. Even in their hustle and bustle, you can observe them peck one another on the mouth as they pass along each other's path. This appears to be some type of affection. Studies show that people who have more affection release more stress-reducing hormones during tense situations than people with very little affection. Showing affection towards others can inspire them as well as contribute to our overall well-being. Respect is a powerful weapon that can be used to build relationships on a daily basis. You can even model the concept to those who have no idea of what it means. This does not give others permission to disrespect or cross your emotional boundaries, but as you sow respect you will reap it as well.

Today's Scripture:

"Therefore, if there is any encouragement in Christ, if there is any consolation of love, if there is any fellowship of the Spirit, if any affection and compassion" Philippians 2:1

JOURNAL PROMPT:

TREATING OTHERS WITH HONOR CAN WORK WONDERS. LIST A FEW WAYS THAT YOU CAN PRACTICE BEING MORE RESPECTFUL. RECORD YOUR IDEAS ON THE JOURNAL PAGE.

Just Be Kind!

"Unity and Love go hand in hand."

DAY 7

"THE GREATEST IN GOD'S KINGDOM ARE THE ONES WHO POSSESS A SERVANT'S HEART. LEADERS SERVE AND CONSERVE."

Ants are thought to be excellent leaders. Ants understand that it's essential to save what they get in the summer, store it up and use it for the winter as they hibernate. This allows them to conserve energy and time. They remember that they cannot go out to get food during the winter season. Their leadership skills don't allow them to consume all they gather at one time. Saving resources is a huge part of their culture. They are natural managers at conserving goods. We have to be good stewards of all that God has entrusted to our care if we are going to be promoted or entrusted with more. Conserve your energy and time wisely by managing these resources diligently. Setting a schedule for the way you spend your money, time, health, relationships, peace, etc will result in maximum utilization and appreciation of your blessings. Purchase a good planner to keep your plans for your goods in front of you. Write your plan on paper as to how you intend to care for your body, soul, spirit, relationships and wealth.

Today's Scripture:

Precious treasure and oil are in a wise man's dwelling, but a foolish man devours it. Proverbs 21:20

JOURNAL PROMPT:

GREAT LEADERS CONSERVE ENERGY AND TIME.
DO YOU HAVE A SAVINGS AND WELLNESS
PLAN? DO YOU HAVE A PLAN TO NURTURE
YOUR RELATIONSHIPS ON A REGULAR BASIS? IF
NOT, RESEARCH WAYS TO IMPLEMENT THEM. IT
CAN BE AS SIMPLE AS TAKING WALKS, HAVING
A DATE NIGHT OR SETTING ASIDE $5 DOLLAR
BILLS EVERY TIME YOU BREAK LARGER BILLS.
INVESTMENTS AND RETIREMENT SAVINGS ARE
ALSO GOOD WAYS TO BE CONSERVATIVE. IF
YOU ALREADY HAVE THESE THINGS SET IN
PLACE, HOW CAN YOU IMPROVE THEM?
RECORD YOUR PLANS AND THOUGHTS ON THE
JOURNAL PAGE.

Value Your
Time.

"

Don't spend all of
the savings at one
time.

DAY 8

"WHOEVER BUILDS UP THE FAMILY, BUILDS UP THE HOME."

Ants diligently build their own home. Though small, ants plan for their own home and they build their own shelters together. Building up your home can be spiritual as well as physical. To "build" means to construct something or to make something stronger. Let's take a valuable lesson from our small friends to work together as families to build each other up and to make home life stronger by working together on issues, projects and goals. Together, we can build our own homes. Praying, planning and working together is everything.

Today's Scripture:

"So then let us pursue what makes for peace and for mutual upbuilding." Romans 14:19

JOURNAL PROMPT:

THE WORD OF GOD TEACHES US TO STIR UP
ONE ANOTHER TO LOVE AND GOOD WORKS. IT
SAYS THAT WE SHOULD NOT NEGLECT TO MEET
TOGETHER. IN WHAT WAYS HAVE THESE
PRINCIPLES BEEN IMPLEMENTED IN YOUR
HOME, CHURCH OR WORKPLACE? HOW CAN
YOU COMMIT TO BUILDING YOUR FAMILY OR
TEAM? RECORD YOUR THOUGHTS OR PLANS ON
THE JOURNAL PAGE.

"If Peace is not in it,
God is not in it."

DAY 9

"YOU ARE STRONGER THAN YOU REALIZE. YOU CAN ACCOMPLISH ANY ENDEAVOR IN WHICH YOU CHOOSE TO ENDURE."

Ants maximize their full potential. Can you imagine how they can accomplish so much? They may appear small and weak, but it quite the opposite. They look feeble but are phenomenal weightlifters. They have great strength and employ great endurance to accomplish the goals that push them to great heights. If God did this for the ant, think about what He wants to do in your life. Stop visualizing yourself as weak and feeble and employ your God-given endurance to accomplish great things. You can lift great weights in the spirit realm and on the earth. Let your prayers focus on gaining endurance and self-confidence. You will receive fresh strength, anointing and grace to move forward in the purposes of God that were created just for you.

Today's Scripture:

"More than that, we rejoice in our sufferings, knowing that suffering produces endurance, and endurance produces character, and character produces hope," Romans 5: 3-4

JOURNAL PROMPT:

THE SUFFERING IN OUR LIVES HAS PRODUCED STRENGTH. YOU ARE STRONGER THAN YOU REALIZE. YOU HAVE BEEN EQUIPPED WITH SUPERNATURAL STRENGTH TO LIFT GREAT WEIGHTS. WRITE ABOUT A TIME IN YOUR LIFE THAT PRODUCED GREAT ENDURANCE, CHARACTER AND HOPE IN YOU WHEN YOU LEAST EXPECTED. RECORD YOUR THOUGHTS ON THE JOURNAL PAGE.

You are Stronger
than you think!

DAY 10

"THOSE WHO WORK IN UNISON CAN RISE TO SEEMINGLY IMPOSSIBLE FEATS"

It is astonishing that ants have so much cooperation and share the same way of communicating in their groups. It is not uncommon to see them working together with one mind and purpose to get a job done. Remember the story in the Bible about the group of people that decided to come together to build a tower that would reach heaven? God had to give them different languages to divert the plan. It was their unison that allowed them to make it as far as they did. If God had not stopped them, they would have achieved this extreme plan. They would have done the unthinkable. What can families and teams do with God-given strategies if they work with a common mind, understand each other's language and have a unified purpose? The unthinkable would happen.

Today's Scripture:

"But the Lord came down to see the city and the tower that the people had started building. And the Lord said, "If as one people all sharing a common language, they have begun to do this, then nothing they plan to do will be beyond them. " Genesis 11:5-6

JOURNAL PROMPT:

SPEAK THE SAME LANGUAGE AS YOUR
SUPPORT SYSTEM. WHAT STEPS CAN YOU TAKE
TO IMPROVE UNITY IN THE FAMILY OR TEAM?
DO YOU ALL HAVE AN "UNDERSTANDING" IN
THE WAY YOU CONVERSE ABOUT GOALS?
RECORD YOUR PRAYERS AND THOUGHTS ON
THE JOURNAL PAGE.

"Nothing can stop two or more united in word and soul ."

Day 11

"THE SECRET TO THRIVING IS A WILLINGNESS TO REMAIN FLEXIBLE"

"Change is the only constant in life" is a famous quote by the Greek philosopher, Heraclitus. There is much truth to this because nothing really remains the same. Our ability to adapt to change is directly related to our flexibility. This quality of bending easily without breaking is the stuff that heroes are made of. Ants have the flexibility to go around, over and under obstacles. As a child, I used to watch in amazement as they climbed great heights to get to an object of desire. We must embrace flexibility as a tool to adapt to the things in life that we have no control over. With God's grace, like the ant, we can learn to maneuver around, over and under unforeseen obstacles without falling completely apart.

Today's Scripture:

"I know how to be brought low, and I know how to abound. In any and every circumstance, I have learned the secret of facing plenty and hunger, abundance and need. I can do all things through him who strengthens me. Yet it was kind of you to share my trouble." Philippians 4:12-14

JOURNAL PROMPT:

ADAPT TO CHANGE THE BEST YOU CAN. WRITE
ABOUT A TIME THAT YOU HAD TO BE FLEXIBLE.
WHAT DID YOU LEARN FROM IT? RECORD YOUR
MEMORIES ON THE JOURNAL NOTES.

Remain *Flexible*
and *Teachable.*

DAY 12

"PATIENCE PAVES THE WAY FOR PRODUCTIVITY"

Ants have natural leadership tendencies that make them finish what they start. They patiently work until the end of the task. Even if they must work in long shifts or take an extremely long time transporting their objects, they don't let it stop them from getting a job done. Let us pray for a commitment to be patient in reaching our targets. If a group of ants can have this mindset, imagine what people could accomplish with this outlook. It does not matter how long it takes, so long as you do not give up. The Word of God teaches that the race is not given to the swift or strong but to the one who endures until the end. Let us press towards the end of our tasks. The more you finish, the faster you can move to the next piece of the puzzle. Patience will ultimately produce productivity. Great understanding belongs to those with patience. Be joyful in hope, patient in hard times and faithful in prayer.

Today's Scripture:

"But if we hope for what we do not yet see, we wait for it patiently". Romans 8:25

JOURNAL PROMPT:

FINISH WHAT YOU START. HAVE YOU EVER
GROWN SPIRITUALLY IN A SEASON THAT YOU
HAD TO BE PATIENT IN? REFLECT ON THIS
SEASON. RECORD THE LESSONS THAT YOU
LEARNED ON THE JOURNAL PAGE.

"Hope for it,
then wait

patiently."

DAY 13

"DEFENSE WILL SAFEGUARD THE EXISTENCE OF THE TEAM"

A team that fights for each other is a team that will overcome anything. Ants work together to fight against threats from outside sources. People, animals, and other ants may come against a colony but not without a fight. Some colonies have been known to create rafts to ensure colony survival during floods! I have always believed in the mantra that teamwork makes the dream work. If our families or businesses work as a unit, it will help protect members during the floods and attacks of our busy lives. In the words of Romans 15:5-6 "May the God of endurance and encouragement grant you to live in such harmony with one another, in accord with Christ Jesus, that together you may with one voice glorify the God and Father of our Lord Jesus Christ." Fight for others by checking on them, praying for them, saying words that build and not break.

Today's Scripture:

I appeal to you, brothers, by the name of our Lord Jesus Christ, that all of you agree, and that there be no divisions among you, but that you be united in the same mind and the same judgment. 1 Corinthians 1:10

JOURNAL PROMPT:

PROTECT YOUR CONNECTIONS. HAVE YOU
EVER MATURED IN A SEASON IN WHICH YOUR
CONNECTIONS SPOKE UP FOR YOU? HOW DID IT
COMFORT YOU? RECORD THESE HIGHLIGHTS
ON THE JOURNAL PAGE.

"A well formed team can birth a well formed

dream."

DAY 14

"COMMUNICATION SETS THE TONE IN THE ATMOSPHERE"

It is a wonder how ants commune with each other. They have some form of communication otherwise they would not flow as well as they do with each other. The word of God instructs us to be quick to hear, slow to speak, slow to anger. These are great guidelines for communication. Verbal and non-verbal communication can make or break relationships and should be taken very seriously. Leaders and followers must be mindful of the listener when sharing steps that make it possible for a vision to manifest. Skilled communication is necessary for all players to win in the game. Ephesians 4:29 warns "Let no corrupting talk come out of your mouths, but only such as is good for building up, as fits the occasion, that it may give grace to those who hear." On the other hand, be willing to receive what others are trying to tell you. Filter it through grace and cut slack so that when it is your time to speak, the ground will be ready to plant on. The bottom line is that people can't read minds, and need to be honored when relaying a message.

Today's Scripture:

When words are many, transgression is not lacking, but whoever restrains his lips is prudent. Proverbs 10:19

JOURNAL PROMPT:

WORDS HAVE A GREAT DEAL OF ENERGY.
ENERGY CAN BE EITHER POSITIVE OR
NEGATIVE. WHAT ARE SOME WAYS OF
COMMUNICATION THAT INSPIRE YOU THE
MOST? DOES YOUR FAMILY OR TEAM
UNDERSTAND YOUR COMMUNICATION STYLE?
DO YOU UNDERSTAND THEIR WAY OF
SPEAKING? RECORD YOUR THOUGHTS ON THE
JOURNAL PAGE.

"Tamed lips can heal many wounds."

A poem inspired by Holy Spirit

I know the ways of the ant,
I own the cattle on a thousand hills,
No one can steal my joy,
know I am GOD and be still,
this is the increase
this is overflow
do it my way
let me run the show
I AM GOD, there is none but me,
I AM like no other
I set the captive free.

Take the Think Like an Ant Challenge!

Use the 3 monthly budget planners and vision sheets on the following pages to focus on productivity. You are more than capable! God designed you to do amazing things. He called you to live an abundant life through His wisdom and grace. As you begin to think more like the ant, you will see growth in every area.

BUDGET PLAN

INCOME		
DATE	DATE	AMOUNT
————	————————	————
	————————	————
————	————————	————

SAVING		
DATE	DATE	AMOUNT
————	————————	————
	————————	————
————	————————	————

EXPANSES		
DATE	DATE	AMOUNT
————	————————	————
————	————————	————
————	————————	————

TOTAL INCOME

BUDGET PLAN

INCOME

DATE	DATE	AMOUNT

SAVING

DATE	DATE	AMOUNT

EXPANSES

DATE	DATE	AMOUNT

TOTAL INCOME

BUDGET PLAN

INCOME		
DATE	DATE	AMOUNT

SAVING		
DATE	DATE	AMOUNT

EXPANSES		
DATE	DATE	AMOUNT

TOTAL INCOME

I can and I will

health

family

relationships

career

personal

my vision board

I can and I will

health

family

relationships

career

personal

my vision board

I can and I will

health

family

relationships

career

personal

my vision board

About The Author

Madra Bell used to think that she had to earn the love of God but He healed her heart and showed her the truth of his grace and unconditional love. She is passionate about inspiring other believers on their walk with christ.

Madra resides with her husband and two daughters, and they have a heart for Jesus. She writes a blog and hosts a devotional podcast each week in which she shares biblical truths, poetry and personal experience.

Her favorite things include flowers, poetry, cooking, decorating, music, nature hikes and dancing. You can find out more about her mission and complimentary resources on her website at madrabell.com.

Notes:

Made in the USA
Middletown, DE
07 December 2022

17193280R00036